Aeolian Harp
volume 4

Edited by Melissa Studdard & Ami Kaye

Guest Editor: Melissa Studdard
Series Editor: Ami Kaye
Project Manager: Royce Ellen Hamel
Layout, Book & Cover Design: Steven M. Asmussen
Copyediting: Linda Kim
Cover Artist: Tracy McQueen

Fonts "National Oldstyle", "Persnickety", and "Metro Thin" designed by Andrew Leman, courtesy of The H. P. Lovecraft Historical Society, www.cthulhulives.org

Aeolian Harp Series: Anthology of Poetry Folios
Volume 4
Copyright © 2018 Glass Lyre Press, LLC
Paperback ISBN: 978-1-941783-48-1

All rights reserved: except for the purpose of quoting brief passages for review, no part of this book may be reproduced or transmitted in any form or by any means, electronic or mechanical, including photocopying, recording, or by any information storage and retrieval system, without permission in writing from the publisher.

Glass Lyre Press, LLC
P.O. Box 2693
Glenview, IL 60025

www.GlassLyrePress.com

Preface

Ami Kaye, Series Editor

The Aeolian Harp series was conceived as a unique platform, one different from a single-author book or literary journal, perhaps something in-between. As a small press we could only publish a limited number of books, but we often read manuscripts with a group of stunning poems that could easily have made up a smaller chapbook or folio. Thus the concept of folios came about: to spotlight poets in a compact format and more intimate setting. The folios offer a selection of each poet's best, most representative work, or a specific series of poems, along with an artistic statement.

A few years back I was fortunate to workshop with Melissa Studdard as mentor and experienced firsthand her flair for creative language, guiding ideas, and refining vision. She is an accomplished poet and editor in her own right, and we are fortunate and grateful for her expertise as guest editor of this volume in the Aeolian Harp series.

We are indebted to to all our submitting poets for allowing us to read and consider their work. In order to select ten folios for this unique publication, we were forced to turn away a quantity of excellent work. The ten folios finally selected offer diverse voices, styles and treatments, and as always, great writing.

Through the ages art and language have reflected our lives, ideals, hopes, and all that makes us human, and in the face of a rapidly changing and threatening world poetry offers an inherent wisdom, beauty and solace. It is our hope readers will find unexpected treasures in the pages that follow.

On a personal note, my father passed away recently following a stroke. He taught me to love poetry, so it seems fitting to quote a couplet from a book he gave me a few years back—Agha Shahid Ali's *Rooms Are Never Finished*:

> After the bones—those flowers—this was found in the urn:
> the lost river, ashes from the ghat, even the rain.

Foreword

Melissa Studdard, Guest Editor

From *Sonnets to Orpheus*

I, 3

A god can do it. But will you tell me how
a man can penetrate through the lyre's strings?
Our mind is split. And at the shadowed crossing
of heart-roads there is no temple for Apollo.

Song, as you have taught it, is not desire,
not wooing any grace that can be achieved;
song is reality. Simple, for a god.
But when can we be real? When does he pour

the earth, the stars, into us? Young man,
it is not your loving, even if your mouth
was forced wide open by your own voice – learn

to forget that passionate music. It will end.
True singing is a different breath, about
nothing. A gust inside the god. A wind.

—Rainer Maria Rilke, trans. Stephen Mitchell

Just as the aeolian harp is often set in a slightly-open window, so we place these poems in our pages to await the gust of your mind. Instruments of beauty, all, they "pour / the earth, the stars, into us" and show us that the breath of true singing emits from many throats. Like harp strings, they vibrate collectively, each making their own sound, together singing the truth of our human experience.

Jocelyn Heath takes us beyond astronomy to a brilliant world "immeasurable by any calculus," a world of "opaque depths" and "tiny solar systems refracted infinitely across the body." The human body, the body of a shell, a black hole—all are imbued with boundless mystery and meaning.

Tanya Ko Hong fearlessly gives voice to those who have been silenced by the physical and psychic traumas of war, depicting the ways war enters and violates the female body and then, "like maple leaf / impressions left on the sidewalk after / they've blown away" or "scars like burnt bark," refuses to leave.

Separating shadow from body, unsticking the soul from a photograph, zeroing in on the eye apart from the face, **Raymond Gibson** defamiliarizes the parts that make us whole so that we may peer "down down down to the depths" and see ourselves and our world anew.

Cynthia Atkins' poems are a bright parade of metaphor and rich detail. Shoes are anarchists, graffiti is a mother, streets are museums, and God is a library. In knowing one object, idea, or emotion, we know another and another and another until the whole world opens before us.

Full of magic and myth, **Jennifer Martelli**'s poems stitch images together so subtly and intuitively that inside her lines I often had the misperception that I was travelling inside my own dream. But, as it turns out, that was not my dream; it was the dream of nature, the dream of the forest manifesting itself as poetry, the dream of tulip bulbs slowing "their memory of bloom."

John James is a poet who reminds us of the incredible flexibility and potential of language. Moving well past the nuance of double and triple meanings, James takes us deep into the music of thought, teasing its rhythms into ever new lyrical formations. Rich with sensory detail and close attention, these poems are a beautiful collaboration of heart and mind.

Holding the reader as captive "between her clasped hands" as the thrush exiled to "a prison of textile," **Shadab Zeest Hashmi**'s ekphrastic sequence is a rich and delightful exploration of how a moment can be captured and preserved brushstroke to canvas, stitch to fabric, artists' imagination to viewer's heart.

Like the alchemist with her stone, **Susan Berlin** transforms the base metal of suffering into the noble metal of personal power. Fierce and brilliant, these poems are electrified by an emotional resilience that gains more and more strength the deeper it plunges into its own vulnerability.

In **Mark Lee Webb**'s poems we find our human story in an unsent postcard, a van packed for a move, cactus thorns used to carve tattoos. It is the story of our relationships with each other and the natural world, a story full of beauty, connection, loss and compassion.

Equal parts sage and poet, **Pamela Uschuk** journeys into the most primal regions of psyche and spirit, returns "as owl breath, as smoke, as wind opening spaces between the brittle branches of winter pines," and leads us gently by the hand to the magical elixir of our own wisdom.

In the preface to *Nine Gates*, Jane Hirshfield reminds us that "poetry's work is the clarification and magnification of being." She writes that "each time we enter its word-woven and musical invocation, we give ourselves over to a different mode of knowing: to poetry's knowing, and to the increase in existence it brings." Through these ten poets we grow larger. Through their breath our own lungs expand. We too are singing, strummed and amplified by the communal knowing of poetry, that great wind.

…this harp which I wake now for thee
　　　Was a siren of old who sung under the sea.

— Thomas Moore, *The Origin of the Harp*

Folios

Jocelyn Heath	13
Tanya Ko Hong	23
Raymond Gibson	35
Cynthia Atkins	43
Jennifer Martelli	53
John James	61
Shadab Zeest Hashmi	75
Susan Berlin	83
Mark Lee Webb	91
Pamela Uschuk	99

Jocelyn Heath

These poems, selected from my manuscript *Veiled Planet*, tell another iteration of the coming-out story through the lenses of the cosmos, our terrestrial environment, and childhood memory. Initially, the potential for cliché in attempting to use the moon and stars rendered so effectively throughout the canon felt too great. But Tracy K. Smith's *Life on Mars* showed me that poets have not yet exhausted the universe as a framework for human concerns. For instance, "Orbital" takes inspiration from a digital representation of the Kepler Project: one dot at each center to represent the sun, and more dots circling on white dotted tracks to show the bodies in orbit. Rows and rows of orbiting bodies against a black screen, spinning like clock gears in endless motion. I thought of the atomic structures we drew in high school chemistry. It struck me as universal synchronicity: we are built of the endless orbits found in the cosmos. We often move around each other as orbiting bodies do their centers, never touching, but by a shift in mathematics, we may just deviate into an unexpected course.

A classmate once asked whether nature had to be so involved in every one of my poems, as it could potentially overtake the ideas themselves. Perhaps, but certainly in works such as "Swallowtails by the Shenandoah" and "Hidden Places," it provides me with my lens of study. Just as formalism served as Adrienne Rich's "asbestos gloves" necessary for handling material too dangerous to treat directly in verse, nature serves as my screen of perception through which I process my own difficult material. In the earlier poems of *Veiled Planet*, space serves this role; in the later sections, I turn to the elements of our terrestrial landscape as the vehicle for exploration. Credit also goes to my wife Michelle, an ecologist, who serves as my living guidebook and fact-checker. She helps me constantly re-see the natural world. Though poet and scientist seek different truths from nature, their shared curiosity leads them both toward discovery, and in doing so, cements their relationship.

Self-Portrait as a Black Hole

Astronomers try to explain me,
but I'm relative like E=m
c², seen only by what accretes near me:
dwarfs, neon gasses, stellar dust like
Einstein's hair veiling his great brain.
Far distant, compressed into my own
gravity, I rotate alone, forcing my
heart to densities
immeasurable by any calculus.
Just step back when it's too much
knotting of space-time to my will,
lest you implode from the pressure—
molten inside—like me.
No one knows what I've taken in:
oxygen the least of it. So many
protons, particulates,
quarks, quirks, and more in a
radius the sharpest radio telescope hardly
sees. That I won't let see—
too many try to solve my mysteries
until they hit dark matter, then
vacillate between us and pleasing the
world. I won't be magnified,
x-rayed, mapped, known by
you or anyone.
Zero divides by nothing.

Orbital

The world encased in celestial glass: God's mobile
on a high shelf, whirling. Taken down, set in the sky

and buoyed across space-time. Man inside, hand pressed
to glass, and in the hand, a microscopic calculus of shells

spins a matched rhythm, seeding flesh hedgerows,
growing the very gardens of us.

Or tiny solar systems refracted infinitely across the body,
their galactic turbulence compressed

the way Krishna parted sandy lips to show the universe perched
on his tongue, half-moon and planets circuiting his palate.

Somewhere, satellites spin into the black, snapping neon
afterbirth of stars growing fast, as gas giants

veer close—then depart on their known orbits,
leaving only moons to keep each other company.

On a street, people push-pull to destinations,
flick open half-spheres of umbrellas

or fall into the metal flow of transit,
joining and separating like shared electrons.

As on a laptop screen, moons swing around planets made of variables,
equations swinging fast or slow, large and small bodies

in wide or narrow circles, some close enough to crash—
others far off and cold, never to touch—

a thousand tiny gears wound to run the universe.

Shell-Gathering in the Keys

Unable to leave one shell unchecked
for flush of cream and flame,
unwilling to break the crouch,
knees cut by mussel shards—

I turn over shell after shell,
drive a thumbnail into the grit
to unearth what's half-buried,
divide shard from scallop.

Down the shore,
a man sweeps his metal detector,
checks every buzz from his wand—
can't help a fifth pass at a spot

knowing how the hand trembles
at the thought of gold
and the overlooked treasure
lodges itself deep.

TOWER

One red bloom
with petals of a child's fingertip's breadth
suspended by a broken trellis over

a concrete square stained with rust,
beside the brief slope flecked
with dust and mica bordering

a kingdom around a vine-wrapped tower.
The blue ribbed doll blanket laid out on a corner
makes a bed. In the beach bucket,

we stir a goulash of leaves and dirt.
My friend imagines that she is a prince
and we lie down,

the double yellow center of the rose
above us an eye leaning ever closer.

Swallowtails by the Shenandoah

A fleet of pale golden sails,
vessels run aground on the river's edge:

two dozen bodies moor to the silt, and
each proboscis threads through the grains,

desperate for the minerals washed
off these Appalachian slopes.

The river's low this year.
Meadows weep dead petals

onto the tongues of cattle.
The hills' shade can't relieve

the longing—the receded shores
paced by countless feet, waiting.

In a week, these dry pebbles
could be submerged or parched.

In two, these butterflies will be
dying as each new chrysalis erupts,

the feather-shine of the fallen
ground into dust.

Hidden Places

Kings Canyon, Australia

Dawn, a lover's searing brush
across sandstone curves,
earth-grooves grow humid
as midsummer swerves

through eucalyptus, born of fire,
swaying its dry dance
while seedpods click
like castanets—

music of sun and shade
and ochre rock,
the tree plays for herself,
the bogong moths, a flock

of honeyeaters shedding
feathers into rainbows
at the canyon's lip
as we start our slow

hike toward the bottom,
brown to orange to white
sediments pressed
by time's tight

hand, split back open.
The air cools
at bottom: an Eden
of deep brown pools,

cycads' squat and ageless
trunks shape a glade
secret as a woman's body,
vine-veiled,

warm and fragrant
stands of grevillea
and earth and leaves.
I enter the water,

draw breath, push
into opaque depths.

Tanya Ko Hong

When I began to write, my focus was validating my own voice as a poet of the Korean Diaspora.

I immigrated from Suk Soo Dong in South Korea, a town where Korean War survivors developed legal and illegal businesses that served an American military base. As a child, I was surrounded by lots of Western culture because of the base, as well as my own culture. Although I was aware of surrounding poverty, my mother provided for us and protected us from the devastating effects of the Korean War. She herself was a survivor of the Korean War, who lost her mother during the war but never told us about her wounds.

I thought that in the United States everything would be forever magical and happy, which was not the reality. I arrived when I was 18 years old and I had a typical immigrant life. The circumstances were hard. Like most immigrants, my father worked two jobs. My mother was left in Korea, and she died before we could reunite.

I had culture shock, I had come from a strict girls school, where students had to wear uniforms, obey the rules and respect teachers and elders. I was taught to be submissive and silent. When I got to America I went to public high school to finish education and it was shocking to see how students behaved. At that time, I couldn't speak English very well. In Chemistry class, I knew how to solve the problems, so I raised my hand, but I didn't know how to explain the answers I knew.

I only recently came to know about Korean 'comfort women,' more than 200,000 women and girls forced into sexual slavery by imperial Japanese before and during World War II. For many years after the war, the comfort women kept silent about their treatment and the subject was taboo until 1991, when Hak Soon Kim became the first woman to go public with her story. I chose to write poems to honor them, speak about their plight and give them their voices.

*Heo Nanseolhean (1563-1589)

If women have *han* in their hearts—

> To be born a woman
> To be born in the Chosŏn Period
> To be the wife of a husband

— frost will come in May.

Father let me study poetry with my brothers
until I married Kim Song Lip and I put it aside.
Waiting for my faithless husband, father said

Write a poem

ask yourself,

Who am I?

---

*Heo Nanseolhean (1563-1589), born Heo Chohui, was a prominent Korean Female poet of the mid Chosŏn dynasty

Grandmother Talking Camptowns

Damn hard work on my back.
GIs pounded and pounded me inside
one day it had to go.
The khanho-won removed my womb
no pension for sex trade
no yungkum.

Before in front of American couple adopted
my half white son—
my half black daughter
I left the orphanage
door.

I had money saved.
My brother stole it
to become a lawyer
I can't protect you he said.
Removed my name from the family
like scraping a baby from the womb.
Still, on birthdays my sister Sook
came secretly with seaweed soup—
Now that she's engaged
Sook cannot return—
She said last,
Why can't you go to America like the others?
I was weeping,
Mother, I wept, mother, we should not live
Let's die together! But Mother is already gone.

The time goes so fast
people on the moon
didn't know where Korea was.

One day I met a man
I made him rice.

He found my American dollars
And never came back.

The War Still Inside You

Tonight my tongue cuts galaxy
black bones be fire
a crying cello drifting
if I open my mouth
I will be sent to the Taklimakan
Desert a graveyard
silence of a thousand skulls
Endless black
Nothing can live
My eyes a flame
I never talk about the battleground
My secret burns there
My silence is your mouth
My skull the house of story
My jaw hinges
stardirt
devastation in a capsule

                                                                    White man said

        No one listens to you
        No one sees
        Open your mouth

I said

            Go ahead.
            Cut and burn my tongue,
            You can't set fire my secrets
            My other tongue.
            has wings
            It will fly

I carry my eyes, my bones
through this war

Oxtail Soup

I look at the bruise on my left hand
    dark purple

mung—holding in the pain
    silence of sorrow
        ashes spread on the ocean
            settling in layers
                palimpsest of lives
                    like maple leaf

impressions left on the sidewalk after
    they've blown away
        a raven on the roof that said
            Disconnect the phone

Turn on the gas
    making Oyako Donburi
    tears come
        cutting up the onions—
            the best gift

I crack cold eggs
    Whip pour over
        boiling napa and chicken broth
            close the pot lid
                turn off the gas
wait

pour over bowl of rice
    feed child—

Empty unmade bed—
    a summer river where
        I didn't want to see his body—

Separation
    one poet said
        after his wife's funeral,
            he found a strand of her hair
                on the pillow and wept

I made sukiyaki the day my dad died—
    I had to feed my children.

Oxtail soup
    That's what Daddy made—
        suck out all the dead blood
            and boil until broth turns milky—

When I leave
I want to leave beautifully.

Comfort Woman

On August 14, 1991, in Seoul, a woman named Hak Soon Kim came forward to denounce the Japanese for the sexual enslavement of more than 200,000 women during WWII. They were referred to as "Wianbu" in Korean and "Comfort Women" in English.

1946, Chinju Again

One year after
liberation,
I came home.
Short hair
not wearing Han Bok
talk without tongue
Mother hid me in the back room

At night Mother took me behind the house
and washed me
Hot steel scars like burnt bark
like roots of old trees
under the crescent glow
She always smiled when she washed me

Your skin is white jade
She bit her lower lip
washing my tummy softly like a baby's
but they ripped opened my womb
with the baby inside

Mother made white rice and seaweed soup
put my favorite white fish on top
  —*but Mother, I can't eat flesh.*

She hanged herself in the granary that night
left a little bag in my room
my dowry with a rice ball.
Father threw it at me
waved his hand toward the door

I left at dusk.

30 years
40 years
forever
mute

bury it with me

>   *They called me, wianbu—*
>   *I had a name.*

1991, 3:00 AM

[That night,
the thousand blue stars
became white butterflies
ripped rice paper,
flew into my room.

Endless white
the web in my mouth,
unhealed red scars,
stitching one by one—
butterflies lifting me
      heavier than the dead
butterflies opening my bedroom door
      heavier than shame.]

At
dawn,
I stand.

Gacela of Moonshine

I want to dance
through war
generations of dark matter
flame my feet burn through
dance like a raven perched on a sand dune.

refuse to numb my dragon heart
do not want to please like lotus
do not want to be a fingerprint
on your thigh

dancing ends at midnight
if the red snake bites your neck
while pomegranate cheeks still burn
you might never get home

Raymond Gibson

Poetry is all the words that resist our indifference and forgetting. There are no magic words; the magic's between the words. The only muses I know are patience and necessity. A poem is neither a story, a speech, nor a song, but resides in the nebulous territory that may overlap any or all of them. There is no right way to make a poem, only however works. And a good poem—if it works—feels quite inexhaustible; makes the reader feel as though they too write it as they read it.

STAGGER INTO DAWN

they slam mirrors shut behind them leaving bare walls
they draw chalk lines around themselves and sink in asphalt

they left their shadows behind holding red balloons by string
fling hands away like gloves mouths open wider than their heads

their teeth dance in beggars' cups while stray buttons stitch up
their guts wrap a sausage of stacked coins and crumbs

they laugh and sob at once or take turns clutching bottles
they hurl hourglasses into the sea as if dust were a message

DEPTHS

you are small
   smaller than lost
like
  an ember among
              stars

you have your
   shadow on dust
time
  this fulcrum of
              bones

you are far
   farther off than
breath
  or light rending
             water

RED NOISE

     I.

dearly departed we are
gathered here   a pile
of   prosthetic limbs on
the white house lawn

     II.

the world went mad
around me and I
tried   to stay sane
learn from the mistake

     III.

bathwater babe in woods
dead   leaves a chewing
noise among verdure's green
flame and copper scent

     IV.

dearly gathered of the
departed here   the words
went   white and prosthetic
limbs house dead noise

GLASS

the naked eye lies
as does the naked
truth water assumes
the shape of its vessel

you see who's in
the door for the frame

eyes have yet to hatch
I am here you are
there or me clothed
in a fold of where

a gem spun like a top
so many lashes clap

THE NEWS

soul came unstuck from its photograph
dust pollinates our silence
hourglass bulbs were once sand too
the crumbs memory ate became birdsong

quotation marks and parentheses still vie for primacy
the stars are so much raining braille
the world is a clock and cracks the dark veins of time
the calendar is a one-sided cage

the weight of a flower crushes death
death is time's surname
honey plastic and vinegar will outlive us
the meaning of life is other people

VIGIL AND PRAYER

so the bell of night lowers
on the flame of day
what nightmare can compare to life
somewhere right now
                        we know
the places but prefer to forget them
as upon waking one dream feeds another

a skull dissevers at the fissures
blooms like a flower
stamens of dull red meld to fire
fever pivots on its brainstem wick

down down down to the depths
the brighter the light the darker the shadow
I can curse the dark while I light a candle
orange speck in the gloaming that I am
may something catch

Cynthia Atkins

I believe in the oppositions the world presents to us—they are critical to our understanding of the world and our experiences in it, these forces that make us function in both the Yin and the Yang of our conditions: the world where we are put in a logical and domestic milieu, only to be thwarted by what Mother Nature serves up to us—what unknowns happen, the things we can't plan on, the weather, how long our life will be, who to invite for dinner. The control we think we have is moot, because everything is clouded by the fates. The natural world is everything that is in flux, change, and in opposition to the control we try to maintain. My writing mostly exists in the yin/yang of interiors, the pathos inside in response to the natural forces of the world. "I tried to drown my sorrows, but the bastards learned how to swim," said one of my great heroes, Frida Kahlo. Misery Must love company, as I think Art is made in the ether world between ecstasy and pain, that place n the hinterlands where most people do not want to vacation. Which is why they say, Artists go in to 'settle the neighborhood.' I write about familial love and all its inherent complexities, as well as mental health, because mental illness is so much a part of my lineage and back ground. If Art is political, this is the way I can contribute and give back to the world.

The cadence of the vowel sounds repeated, making a pattern, a line break that furls into a juicy enjambment— these are the quirky and idiosyncratic strokes and moments at craft that challenge and give me a lot pain and pleasure. Trying to engage with words and making them mean and say something more than I am capable of saying in my every day speech to another human being. "A poem is really a kind of machine for producing the poetic state by means of words," said Paul Verlaine. I guess what I am saying is that for me part of what people go to *Religion* for is what I go to poetry for—Jettison the material world for a while and ask the deeper questions, and poetry is my way in.

The Street is A Museum

And all the shoes are anarchists wanting real earth.
My own shoe-strings of luck, gone south. Mine is
the face that holds breakable bones, inside a church
of moans. The party-goers left stain-glass fragments
and late night whispers, smoky and vengeful
with buyer's remorse. A coin-toss of loss
and old cassette tapes. Gnarled as Hell and
plastic threads are the filaments through nests.
Smelling of hot donuts, cigar smoke, late-night
mutterings. I think my ancestors live
in the branches, how they twirl to the klezmer
music—like a horse tail snapping in a gust of wind.
The sound of their voices fat as a school bus squealing
the breaks in rain. Grandmother, aunt,
cousin, uncle—I let them stamp their 'madness stain'
upon my arm. Once I pressed a leaf in a book
and it rested like a birth mark—It carries me
into the kitchens where the maelstrom of life
happens. *But no, you can't have my son,
good night, I love you,* stinging in the doorway.
I've walked through a few puddles to get to
the clouds, where there were door knobs
and wayward stars calling my name.

God Is A Library

If you look under G in the card catalog,

a hunched-over landlady will rent you

a space made of dust, albeit, a little domain

of quiet— Where the rent is cheap and so

is the debt, and silence is not morbid.

On these premises, text and rhetoric

mix a sexy playground for words.

Exquisite human machine of pathos

and debris, allowed the pages to be set

on letter-press, then ink bled and seeped

into a refinery of senses. The kids practice

spelling in the back stacks. We are all polar-opposites

on a stage of belief, fact and faith. Yes, Borges

digressed for an atheist and an Aleph. Delinquent,

these prophets and scholars broke the dress-code

in favor of *out-of-fashion souls*. Under the desk,

two students knock knees to make contact.

Egg to sperm, pen to pulp—Ideas fly to where

our better angels reside—Where chairs are stacked

on tables at the end of the day.

Graffiti Is My Mother

She lay on her back

Brick by rail by brick—

Her wheels rilling lullabies

With rubber and rust—Drawn

In chalk, gone when rain comes.

A time once upon, I was made

from rubble—A frail cocktail

of biology and troubled luck.

I am the neighborhood

of stairwells, a bird wing-patched

in safety pins and raw databases

of cement. Don't lament, Mother—

In my eyes, in my handwriting,

In the faces on milk cartons—

We count the holes in heaven.

You left the stars in a purse

and I am that vessel of teeth

and bone. A fire-escape

of language skipping me

all the way home.

FAMILY THERAPY (II)

We ignore the kinship of strangers
because we are seamed and stitched
together—our canopy for the long haul.
      This pathos has static and is stuck
like the plastic covers in the photos albums.
We are composed of posed facts
and time eludes us with
      Country Club smiles.
I wore patent leather shoes and polka-dot
socks from the bargain basement
of the Family unmentionables.
      In collusion, the hand-me-downs
have given birth to aunts, uncles,
and the rowdy cousins. My Family
needs an accountant for the bank
of DNA—which stands for,
      Do Not Abandon
Ship. We come from a long line
of liars and fools running off
with the silver— Because we are
Family, our inkless shadows
      have left no prints.
Let's recast the time when Aunt June
knocked on the back door, unannounced—
a wilted flower in her wilted couture.
      No worse for wear, all the way
from Miami, she came to bellow and shriek
like a freak teapot. Theory: Aunt June clocked
a few degrees south of center—
reviving our ancient fear that all roads
      lead to Florida.
This elevator is already full, thank you,
so I keep looking for a balcony
from which to drop. The Family

is worried to death
that there are no happy endings.
But when push comes to shove,
our shadows will always make room
    for the next of kin.

Zig-Zag

Don't worry, you'll know me
I'll be the one crouched beside myself—
Jewish Yankee in a Southern town.
I'll be the one saving for the next life—
    My folded grocery bags
      could extend for miles.
Bear with me, I'm saying this
for the last time—
I had been service orientated.
    I was the subject
of an experiment in derision—
    The sum total, splitting apart,
unrecognizable as a flea. I put out
    an all-points-bulletin,
but still couldn't find myself.
    I can't draw a straight line
for the life of me. But really, I don't want
your sympathy. I'll wait my turn. I know how
    to suffer, that part is easy—
I'll be the one with my hands
 to my ears— right before a china cup
    hits the tile floor. My head gathered
as a small, angry crowd. By and by, my sister loosed
her sanity like a glove. I've faked and faked it well.
    I hear our ancestors yelling
from the mental ward of hell. We are right to be afraid.
It's the job we're here to do. I'll be the one
    with my hands up in the air—
But then, how will I know you?

God is the Myth

—"What cannot be said will be wept."—Sappho

Not for the sheepish or the faint of heart—Every day

we mark the calendar with one more hangnail of grief.

I shivered on a porch swing, locked out of

my house, donning a terrible secret.

Owned and handled, I stood sedate

as a police out-line. My past until this moment

is penciled in the way an artist suggests a cloud.

This is the narrative—repeat it, repeat after me.

I never existed before this moment.

Under a stairwell, I could feel my fear

like skin caught in a zipper. The last touch

of red on the artist's brush. I heard many cries,

like scrawny cats in the alley of my heart.

My swagger was black and blue and smacked-up

with pool hall chalk. Now, a civil anguish that

ransacked homes like weeds in the sidewalks.

A militant boot in the face of every word. The gods

are lactating in stone. So this is what I did, proof

I was here on this rocky turf—Sketched this narrative

of cardinal sin and madness. Careless sleuth

of testimony, I set this self on paper. There I caught

a glimpse of my old aunt brushing her hair,

her wrist was inked and numbered. I built a fort

out of fabric and rubber tires. A thunderclap

to light the wholly and fearless Interior.

Jennifer Martelli

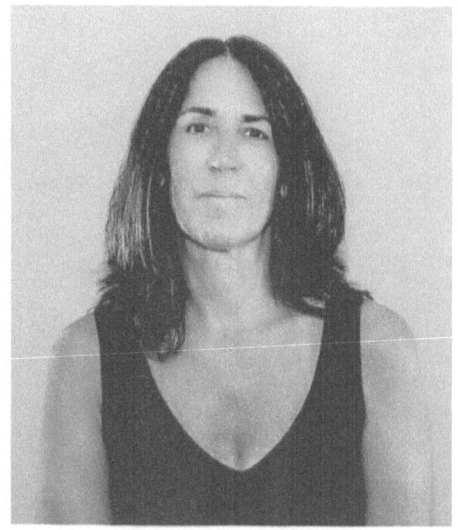

Much of my writing is about women: relationships between women, with men, children, and in the shadow of our political situation, society. I grew up the middle daughter of three girls, so I am comfortable in—and fascinated by—a female world.

"Pluto's Heart is a White/Shadow" was written the summer they re-instated Pluto as a planet. I was playing with the idea of women transforming into flying creatures (I got this idea from the film "A Girl Walks Home Alone At Night" which featured a skateboarding vampire in a burka who looked like a beautiful bat).

"Phoebe," is a poem about love and recovery.

"Mal 'Occhio"—This is an Italian term for "evil eye," which is the curse of envy.

The poems, "Winter is for Women," "The Nightingale and The Finch," and "The Sacrifice" were all written as responses to Sylvia Plath poems. I took part in The Plath Poetry Project, which followed the calendar of Plath's *Ariel* poems.

"Winter is for Women" is a response to "Wintering." I loved the accumulation of food in the pantry, as if for survival, as well as the claustrophobic feeling. The title is a line in the poem—stark, relaying a way of being. I loved her line, "Her body a bulb in the cold and too dumb to think," which reminded me of my Queen of Night bulbs!

"The Nightingale and The Finch" responds to Plath's "Winter Trees," as well as to the #MeToo movement. The nightingale, in myth, was Procne, a victim of rape who had her tongue cut out; her sister was transformed into a finch.

"The Sacrifice" is a response to "The Bee Meeting," one of my favorite poems. I tried to respond to Plath's distrust and agony. Plath's Bee Sequence is terrifying: a dangerous and empowering world in her last year.

Winter is for Women

—"Wintering," Plath

The Queen of the Night bulbs arrived from Holland in a mesh bag

tucked into a perforated box: one American dozen dying to breathe our air.

They looked like twelve moons of an outer planet named after a god:

airless & misshapen & demanding to be part of our orbit. In their split

hearts, these women grip their toxin & beauty in a tight fist, know exactly

what they're capable of: stigma & stamen & black silk leaves complete &

tucked & folded like the shadow moths on the back screen door.

The tulip bulbs know what's inside better than Christ did of the mustard seed.

They've no use for faith.   My friend says to bury them now

or shut them in deep cold, in the freezer with sacks of golden niblet corn &

blocks of butter, savory broth, basil down cellar where even the cats won't go—

they need to lie dormant, sleep dreamlessly, slow their memory of *bloom*.

Pluto's Heart is a White/Shadow

The dogs tonight don't hang in the warm sky. Snouts up
they howl in their homes, against the drawn shades.

Hungry silhouettes. They bay: want want want
or warn warn warn. But what do I know of dog Morse code?

Tonight, a cancer grows under a burka or habit or tichel scarf.
A bat or vesper dove or gray owl flies past the pearl moon.

My friend is a Cancer and walks sideways, like a crab, looks me in the eye.
Sidle, she says, *hang onto the apogee, reach wide with your arms.*

The Nightingale and The Finch

Neither abortions nor bitchery—"Winter Trees," Sylvia Plath

The white birches stand solid: jock legs
circled up with a plan in a grove at dusk,
paper skin covered in knotty dark eyes.

A nightingale flies around the trunks, the gold
frozen molted skin of a long snake
caught in her beak flutters, a flag conquered.

The nightingale won't ever again be called bitchy:
she has neither tongue nor teeth. She grinds her food
with stones, grinds it soft, scrapes clean her gut:

she'll never seek an abortion. She doesn't sing
or weep or tell. She'll weave the snake's skin
into her nest, make it shimmer. Her sister is a finch.

She follows the gleam of skin through the grove to give
three small feathers, blue speckled chips from the curve
of the broken eggshell, a song. My friend asks me when

I'll stop writing about the birch trees.
When they stop looking at me.

Phoebe

says, I was up in the room by the trees making my girl's bed and I could still smell her sleep. When I snapped the sheet, starlings, ten thousand it seemed, rose from the old larch all at once, settled, rose again and flew off. And then I lay down. But only my body slept, something else was awake but trapped. The bowl on my table is filled with blood oranges which, during Advent, are un-gassed green and sweet and five for a dollar. I peel a section off my own (it sighs like a red bird's lung) and offer it to her. She takes my hand. I've given over all the easy things—the envy and greed, but not what I love: my daughter, my life. How do I do that? Let go of what I love? She opens her palm and points to the crescents etched on the seams with her gibbous moon fingers. Don't tell anybody this. It's mine.

Mal'Occhio

Last night the new moon bloomed
the green leaves

on my backyard maple,
urged the tiny glow worms

down from their silk threads
onto the oxidized

eaves of the feeders.
The vernal pool dug out

from the broken sidewalk
had an airtight seal

of pollen: nothing could survive.
I'd gone to sleep

envious. I woke
to the news: a brutal

man hanging from a cotton noose
in his cell. None of this

was in my mind. The birds
circling since before the day broke—

even they were starved.

The Sacrifice

why am I cold?—"The Bee Meeting," Plath

Nobody knows it's me.
I am wearing a full-grown doe's head.
I took the cut crystals from the chandelier,
hung them from my birch-branch antlers.
I am wearing her pelt (not real, golden
felt squares patched & stitched
myself). Nobody feels unsafe.
My eyes are slit like my cats',
like the eyes of the small amber goat,
pure velvet slit.
I wanted to wear my Anjou pear
costume, the velour purple one
& hide in the branches of the tree outside
the house that is having the party.
I wanted to bruise easily like fruit
left fallen under the trees in autumn.
There wasn't a color close enough—
not really blue, not the color of a dull
knife tarnished, not the tarnish,
not the color of the lead core
of a pencil. Not the color of skin
under the eyes of a menstruating woman.
I want to dress as a narrative—an arc
the shape of a breast, the good one
that grows over a heart in a rib cage.
The whole town gathers to watch
in a field of sweet grass.
Now I am milkweed silk.
My skin, soft as burnt butter.
Betrayal by one is betrayal by all,
by the whole town red

blushing stomach sac, deep &
strewn as a pomegranate.
Here is the mid-fall altar. Here is the body.
Here it is swollen & shamefully warm.

John James

Poetry, for me, is a tool for thought: a method of critiquing social structures and interrogating ideologies that imagines a just and more tenable future. While poetry traffics in convention, the best poems upend such forms, estranging readers from their preconceived notions of subjectivity and permitting new modes of apprehension.

I am particularly interested in the notion of hypertextuality, a poem's ability to engage with, excerpt from, and build on other texts. The term "hypertext" was coined in 1965 by the computer scientist Ted Nelson and signifies a text containing links to other texts, a defining feature of the Web. By juxtaposing passages with diverse histories that operate in distinct linguistic registers, I experiment with voice and texture, creating poems that are not only polyphonic but that fashion a model of connectivity useful for understanding the technologies and ecologies my poems explore.

This is especially true of "History (n.)," which excerpts language from journalistic and philosophic texts to mimic the relentless sensory input characteristic of smart phones and new media. Other poems delve more concretely into biography. "Chthonic" employs a loose surrealism to consider the intersection between consumer culture and the intimate spaces of quotidian experience ("The feathers / in my pillow came / from a factory in Beijing") but also to meditate on my father's death. The title derives from the Greek *khthon*, which refers to that which is below the earth's surface: originally, it meant the mythological Underworld, but in its colloquial sense, it might signify archeological artifacts, root systems, microbe ecologies, or the dead. The process of uncovering these items is the process of uncovering histories, personal and collective.

Additionally, my poems juxtapose an interest in burgeoning technologies with an interrogation of the nature-culture dialectic central to our era of climate disaster. By modeling the very ecologies they seek to describe, my poems grapple with a clash between aesthetic and political forms endemic to poetry as such. In this vein, not only do my poems dislodge readers from positions of familiarity and comfort, they strive to imagine the world-shaping change necessary for sustainability in the Anthropocene.

Years I've Slept Right Through

The field is steeped with the violence of horses.
Night descends blue hills
and I attempt to weigh distance,
as a calf tests its footing to the water-hole.
On the front porch, my cat devours a hummingbird.
He beats the brilliant body with his tufted paws.
He breaks its wings,
swallows whole the intricate bone-house.

Inside, the pilot light is burning.
My sister's friend with the coal-eyes is over.
Gradually, I crawl into bed, aching for more light.
In the dooryard
a young boy stoops to pluck
feather from feather until his hands are sore.
So prone to sadness, this thief—
I take my glasses off and lay them on the table.
The shadow of a tree rests inside my palm.

This spring I commemorate my father's death
by tacking deer-horns above the door.
My hammer-strokes disperse
an assembly of hens,
waiting around for me to scatter their seed.

A mile away the river is abundant.
It breaks its sudden excess
on a limestone bridge.
A big-axled wagon tips into the water,
where white mud washes the coachman clean.
This is a custom he repeats every year,
coming and going until his wheels give out,
coming to wet his tongue.

Dawn chalks over the horizon
rendering the sky a storm-blotched red.
The outline of a cow appears on the hill,
and then dissolves into the fog.
I follow her path with my ear,
listening as a bell sounds out the trail—
It is mine, this world
of bread and skin and stone.
Lay me in the field with all the fallen horses.

History (n.)

"I didn't make these verses because I wanted to rival that fellow, or his poems, in artistry—I knew that wouldn't be easy—but to test what certain dreams of mine might be saying and to acquit myself of any impiety, just in case they might be repeatedly commanding me to make this music."

—*Plato, Phaedo*

Viewed from space, the Chilean volcano blooms.

I cannot see it. It's a problem of scale. History—the branch

of knowledge dealing with past events; a continuous,

systematic narrative of; aggregate deeds; acts, ideas, events

that will shape the course of the future; immediate

but significant happenings; finished, done with—"he's history."

—

Calbuco: men shoveling ash from the street.

Third time in a week. And counting.

Infinite antithesis. Eleven

miles of ash in the air. What to call it—

just "ash." They flee to Ensenada.

—

The power of motives does not proceed directly from the will—

a changed form of knowledge. Wind pushing

clouds toward Argentina. *Knowledge is merely involved.*

Ash falls, it is falling, it has fallen. *Will fall.* Already flights

cancelled in Buenos Aires. I want to call it snow—

what settles on the luma trees, their fruit black, purplish black,

soot-speckled, hermaphroditic—*if this book is unintelligible*

and hard on the ears—the oblong ovals of its leaves.

Amos, fragrant. Family name *Myrtus*. The wood is extremely hard.

—

        Ash falling on the concrete, falling on cars, ash

        on the windshields, windows, yards. *They have lost*

        all sense of direction. They might as well be deep

        in a forest or down in a well. They do not comprehend

        the fundamental principles. They have nothing in their heads.

—

The dream kept

    urging me on to do

what I was doing—

    to make music—

since philosophy,

    in my view, is

        the greatest music.

—

History—from the Greek *historía*, learning or knowing by inquiry. *Historein* (v.) to ask. *The asking is not idle.* From the French *histoire*, story. *Hístor* (Gk.) one who sees. *It is just a matter of what we are looking for.*

Metamorphoses

what was it this
morning : you said

redgrass glistens
in surf : the pine

board fence collapsed
along the line : after

the storm a kestrel
in headwind : sand

accumulates on your
feet : puckered seal

skin : the salt-washed
flesh : wreckage towing

upshore : when the
gulls came out I saw

them circling in air :
saw them pecking

seals' eyes from
torn skin : a boy

downstrand rolling
in dunes : I could see

the stomach's red
wall : the small hairs

on its flippers : blubber
wretched by shark

bite from the belly's
swell : later seen

from a dune : black
water : fish spit

pooling : mouth open
enough to see teeth

trailing in sand : his lips
limp : there in

the storm's wake
I wanted something

to say : the ocean
scraped his insides clean

The Milk Hours

>   *for J.E.J., 1962-1993
>   and C.S.M.J., 2013-*

We lived overlooking the walls overlooking the cemetery.
The cemetery is where my father remains. We walked
in the garden for what seemed like an hour but in reality must
have been days. *Cattail, heartseed*—these words mean nothing to me.
The room opens up into white and more white, sun outside
between steeples. I remember, now, the milk hours, leaning
over my daughter's crib, dropping her ten, twelve pounds
into the limp arms of her mother. The suckling sound as I crashed
into sleep. My daughter, my father—*his son.* The wet grass
dew-speckled above him. His face grows vague and then vaguer.
From our porch I watch snow fall on bare firs. Why does it
matter now—what gun, what type. Bluesmoke rises. The chopped
copses glisten. Snowmelt smoothes the stone cuts of his name.

Poem Around Which Everything Is Structured

On his third night of dreams the boy turning in his bed
        hums about goodness & trees. He sees the berries
in his palm, which are the final berries of the season,

        so he squeezes them to watch their juice bleed through
the dim crevasses of his hand. Something's missing
        in this song & I don't know what it is. A shadow, maybe,

or a light between trees. Tonight, as the stars seep
        through his window & touch the dusty water he keeps
sitting in a glass by his bed, the boy wonders what it would be

        to touch the body of another. I search his eyes
for mutual absence. And maybe as I map the freckles
        on his wrist, as the song crescendos, as the night fades into

dull purples & blues—maybe the lights go out & I feel
        his breath on my hand. Or maybe that's wrong, too.
Maybe I become the delicate prison he attends to, the cold

        thread wending in & out his chest, the rapture he feels
when he dangles me from the wood post of his gallows.
        Suppose I wrote this song in another key entirely.

I could cast it in a way that doesn't care about touching
        & hips. The boy could carry a spade out into the yard
& drop it down into the soil, where the earth would dance

        around it & the stars shrink into the distance until they
disappear between hills. This is how I think, Love,
        about you. This is how I structure everything around me

that needs to be structured—the taste buds on your tongue,
      the salt of your wrist, the shape of your mouth as you
tell me every little thing you ever wanted me to know.

      I want to give him a name, that boy. I want to call that name
on nights when the ceiling hangs low above my bed,
      & the plaster cracks, & the sky pokes through the minute

slits between blinds. I want to feel his hands, not my hands,
      shivering in the wool sleeves of my coat, anything
but the same shaking of the leaves, the orchid dying bloom

      by bloom in the window while its naked stem bends
a single blossom toward the sun. It delights in a small
      cool mist. Let me speak plainly. Let me get to the dark

heart of the matter. The thing is, Love, that when I watch
      the squash buds wither, when the June sun makes them
shrivel into themselves, it's almost too much for me to bear.

      I see them—& that is all. I hear an emptiness in the wind,
& wrap my mind around it, & think of the king snake coiled
      in the grass. Soon he will be skin & bones. Already he is but

skin & bones. He rubs his head against a rock. The sun shines.
      Wood lice creep from the open dirt. Tonight, as the boy
turns in his bed, & wrestles with the prospect of his own

      approaching dusk, I bend myself above you, or below, whichever
way it is that you prefer. I breathe the clean grasses
      of your skin & unpack each assorted item you keep hidden

in a travel sized box by your purse. And I, & the boy, sit
      blinking in the dark, staring off at the wall & the dead stars
beyond it throwing cold light through the black matter

      of millennia. It rests inside his palm. It rests in mine. At times,
looking out at the bare sky, & watching those stars fizzle
      in the map of still time, I want to crawl up into its stillness,

& feel obsolete, distant from my father & the warm bodies
      I've touched, & watch through a tree so lovingly hollowed
their vague shapes flit between leaves. It's a problem

      in philosophy & form, each hand's different twenty-
seven little bones reaching out to hold the cloth
      draped upon the shoulders of another. Slowly,

those shapes come into focus, & the dawn light, which is
      not dead light, seeps into the room. In it, in the yard,
where the boy throws down his spade, & a mule-tailed deer

      licks dew from his palm, the apple trees shine, collard
stalks stiffen, the paper-white bark of an aspen
      quivers, Love, & the grasses shudder in unison, in wind.

CHTHONIC

My light bulb is gone.
        It was dying anyways.
The room goes dark
        before I sleep. I lie
eyes closed, listening,
        hoping the radio waves
cause only one type
        of sick. My bed's
not safe. The feathers
        in my pillow came
from a factory in Beijing.
        Their birds fly east
in the shape of a *V*.
        On the edge where
my mother sat reading
        a bright picture book
something has taken
        her place. My father's
mouth, which I lost
        years ago, speaks
from a jar on the shelf.
        I ask my mother
what she did with the light.
        She says it's
under the bed. I ask
        my father why
he can't hear. He tells
        me he's underground.

Shadab Zeest Hashmi

How do artifacts absorb stories of empire? How is art employed (or deployed) to shape cultural narratives? What happens when elaborate symbols of power collide with the power and grace of simpler human experiences of art and existence? These are some of the questions I explore in my new manuscript, based on the history of empire and aesthetics, trade, war and cultural interactions along the ancient "Silk Route," a geographical area which extended from East Asia to Europe— much of which has been a scene of war, imperial and economic power struggles shaping the arts and cultural narratives of our times.

"Empire Ekphrasis"(published in Mudlark, 2017):

In this series of poems, I see works of art and music through the filter of imperial history and I attempt to find contrasts between the impression of indulgence reflected in an empire's sensibility and its paucity of connection with the larger beauty and spirit of ordinary life. While art may boast and boost the power of an empire, and empire may afford (some) artists the luxury to indulge in art for art's sake, the history surrounding the aesthetic language of empire, especially the history of oppression, resides in it permanently as a haunting presence. The works included in this series are: Strawberry Thief, a well-known fabric design by William Morris, paintings A Mughal Prince with his Falcon (India, Mughal Empire, unknown artist, circa 1600-1605), Sheikh with the Tiger by Rudolph Ernst, The Awakening Conscience by William Holman Hunt, and the musical piece "Prelude to the Afternoon of a Faun" by Claude Debussy, (after Stéphane Mallarmé's poem).

"Hawa is love that shares its name with "air" and "falling" (a section from "Saif ul Malook" published in Papercuts Magazine, 2015):

is a narrative poem based on the Pakistani legend of Saif ul Malook— the enchanted lake where fairies come to bathe under the night sky. In the story, when prince Saif visits the lake and falls in love with the fairy-princess Badar and saves her from a demon, she agrees to marry him. But when the marriage requires compromise, it is not Saif but Badar, a creature of fire and air, who sacrifices her wings in order to live in the palace as his queen. She soon realizes that it was not a sound decision; she flies away, causing Saif to pursue her and ultimately learn the value of love and sacrifice.

I visited the lake as a child and heard the story, wondering what it must be like for a fairy to try to conform to a wingless, flightless life. As an adult, the feminist conclusion of the story is all too apparent.

Strawberry Thief Singing

The thrush, _{caught} jubilant, after stealing
ripe fruit from the artist's garden, goes to
a prison of textile, serves a sentence
of centuries in cotton, needles passing
through her feathers, stiches on the sigh
(or the ghost of song) in her bill, on wings.
She will be stretched on raj furniture
across the commonwealth, a souvenir
in chintz, her crime displayed on bedspreads.
She will hang from windows, a doll of the wind.

A Prince and his Falcon

The Mughal brushstroke is thirsty for hunt
Mares, moonlit steppes, skull heaps, coils of Mongol
destiny come back as Indian henna tendrils,
geese, cheetahs, antelopes embroidered
on a prince's tunic, sword sweating falsities
tied with a brocade sash. The prince, vacuous,
the shape of a question, the falcon, impenetrable;
its metallic gaze humiliating
golden tassels wrapped around its leather
perch, plumage full, mass of unbidden history

The Four Horns in the Afternoon
of a Faun,

two bassoons, three flutes, two harps, oboes
Plus the heat of strings at midday, cirrus,
that squirrel-colored wisp of cloud curling
around the faun, leaves nothing to chance,
each blade of grass is art-hungry, upturned
to receive a dewy gem fattened by
slender nymphs. A man, golden as goat,
beast of meadows, a climber who shears
innocence to fabricate innocence,
goes on crowning himself, girdled by dream

The Sheikh and the Tiger,
having just offered prayers

sprawl on the cavernous, velvety shelf
of the Orientalist's fantasy
There are no charming constrictors,
lutes or water-pipes snaking between empire
and voyeur, but a curious Sheikh with skin
a shade less copper than the tiger, both
beast and beast stretched in ultimate luxury
on the prayer carpet. The sheikh in diaphanous
silk has somehow exited the sacred moment with
one arm bare, muscular, sinister—etched in the future

The Awakening Conscience swaddled in red Cashmere

panics, rises from empire's lap, finds you,
dear viewer, between her clasped hands, and you,
doused in cold sweat, have only a mirror
behind her to show you light from the window
ghosting through trellis and tree. Time, in
sudden primal shame, stands naked under
a glass dome on the blustery piano.
She steadies herself, feet between empire's limp
glove and the spasm of wings— the feline grasp
unlocked. Window: a giddy call echoed by mirror

Hawa is love that shares its name with "air" and "falling"

Flying, flailing, falling. The fairy beats her wings
She is of a fire that seeks the cool of the lake
The man is of clay, seeks the shade of a pine,
leaves geometry, archery, oratory, grammar,
leaves the comfort of reason
Her pulse is a bolt of lightning
His dream is a field of tulips
She leaves her wings by the lip of the lake
He leaves his share of freedom under briars
Creature of fire, creature of dust: *explain water*

Susan Berlin

Being math-averse, I planned to major in Psychology, until I found out that Statistics was a required course. So I moved in another direction – but psychology has always remained a strong focus point.

Also: people. I like poems that have people in them, and bits of conversation. In many poems, I'm searching for answers as to what makes us who we are, why we do the things we do. Often, motive and ulteriority come into play. (I also wanted to be a detective).

Someone asked me recently: Who do you write for? And instantly I recalled, from 20 years back, the shampoo girl at the salon where I used to go who was crying as she worked the suds on my head into a lather, telling me about her recent divorce and how much she still loved him — being completely open, exposing her pain to a complete stranger, withholding nothing. Her tears erased her makeup, creating white stripes down her face. After blowing her nose, she turned her focus to me, asked me what I do and said she'd never read a poem, didn't think she'd like them much.

At home, I wrote a poem. It was about her. I brought it with me, next time I went. She took it to the back of the shop where black plastic capes hung like oversized bats from a strip of hooks near the coffee maker and stacks of upside-down Styrofoam cups. Holding the paper by the edges with both hands as if something holy, she sat facing the mirrored wall to read it, closed her eyes, read it again.

When she came out front, the stylist was blowing my hair dry, making small talk difficult. The shampoo girl handed me back the poem, folded now, bent down to whisper in my ear: I do nails, too. I unfolded the paper. In the lower right corner (drawn in nail polish) a stout little heart in a bold frame and, beneath it — in gold glitter — her signature. It's the first time she told me her name.

To be honest, I write for her.

False Witness

There must have been some good in him,
but all I remember is our father calling every
now and then to say he's getting married

again and would Bobby and I care to come.
True, there was that one time he spent the entire
day with us, those pictures he took:

the front of the bus with its grimy promise
of Coney Island; the green mildewed boats
that moved slow enough to go around

only once; Bobby and me in pea-coats, collars up
against the off-season gusts, back-dropped by various
games of chance. There's that shot with our heads

cocked at the same strained angle, our lips
puckered like fish, pulling at the cotton candy's
sticky mass. And then

all the exposures he took – the remainder
of the roll – of rides we didn't go on,
restaurants where we didn't eat.

The Armoire

My parents kept getting bigger
houses as if more space would allow them
to hate each other less. The last place
we lived, my father left my mother alone
in the master bedroom and moved himself
into the spare. Nothing treasured there —

a tired cot, a vinyl ottoman with one
short leg — but the antique armoire and what
it stored: white linens and bed sheets,
hand-stitched, and, along the borders,
red tulips embroidered with light
green leaves. These, he lugged

to the basement, dumped them on the bag
of lime used for killing weeds. Once, when
the need to know what he held sacred
made my mother enter his room, she approached
the armoire and slowly opened its arched
gothic doors: on nothing, nothing inside

but emptied bottles of men's cologne
and a wall calendar not meant for any nail,
the square of each day of each month
crossed out by a thick black X,
including the month they were in
and half of the next.

Through the Funnel of a Loose Fist

Climbing the stairs after the argument,
she sees her husband sideways,
crouched near the bookcase.

With one finger, he hooks the crinkled edge
of a book's binding and tilts it towards him,
rocking it out of place like an old dog's tooth,
adding this one, too, to the tower he's built
without first flipping open the cover
to see who owns it. Words

dissolve like Eucharist on her tongue
as she returns to the kitchen where the wind,
sibilant hours ago through a crack in the caulking,
has now settled down. She fills the kettle
with little more than half an inch
and, while waiting for it to whistle,

transfers the cashews he loves
from the leaf-shaped dish
into a tightly-lidded jar.

Prayer

deargod dear God dear
barking dog in the neighbor's yard
dear staked birch staccato heart dear
rabid raccoon trapped between ceiling and roof   all religions
are true they all my son swears say
the same thing in different ways   so does it
matter what I call you   should I say Lord
or god or mother or wind   dear dead
brown leaf holding
to the windowscreen like a moth   should I
roll back the rug so my knees bare
against the hard floor
will hurt more am I saying this right   I mean
I've seen the old women in black shawls
at the shrine of Guadaloupe
crawling on their knees in the heat
leaving pale pink dots on the concrete
then larger spots   cardinal red
on the path leading to the marble steps   and the black-robed priests who
grab their arms and raise them to their feet
but blind faith is   Greek to me
so what's the pecking order
the etiquette here   must an atheist's daughter
pray more than a baptized son   a former friend   born
again with one hand on my head proclaimed in a tone
certain of being heard   a list of demands   things for You to do
on my behalf saying
And, Lord, make her prosper in every way
when my only request
was just   to let my mother   live
another day

Request Denied

At the end, no one showed but us:

distant daughter, twice-disowned son
and Wife #6, cracking gum, practicing
your signature on your last withdrawal slip.
Who else did you think would come?
From what source a guest list drawn, a crowd

to rally as you sank, yacht-sails dragged through
water you fouled? Perhaps a priest to anoint
you, proud atheist, on your way down? Maybe
Wife #4, bearing a basket of fruit and the knife
she tried to stab you with? Or would you prefer
to take the 5th?

Which of your siblings, long deleted from
your mailing list, did you expect to make the trip,
to cough up six bucks for gas, plus tolls? And which
of us (your two children, known) owed you so much
as an hour of our grown-up time, you who never
held a hand or gave a dime?

Hard to admit — country-club Communist
short-tipping your caddy, sweet-timing
saccharine sugar daddy, buttering your way
in and out of wedding rings (more than enough
for one entire hand). In the end, even you
wanted tears and a 6-piece band.

How poorly you planned.

Poem Not to be Read Aloud

:

Because today   this day   moon-sun-moon
  some woman   girl mother maiden aunt
is tying   knotting taping binding
  a bundle   letters poems
                  knitted clothes for a stillborn child
and hiding it   (   )
  where some day   ?/?/?
someone may
  discover   uncover unbury find
         it

Because the bundle's weight doubles when it's bound

Rip   sever burst split
  whatever binds
Bite the fruit   flesh seeds rind
  re-write your name
Hold your words up to
  a thousand mirrored doors   opening out
Listen   to the untwisting of the twine

 because this
is that woman's story   whisper song
  and my mother's   secret bundle buried under
and   what is of me
              what I own
        that to which I belong

and not   not going
  not going to be

      mine

Mark Lee Webb

In my poetry, I start with the observed world and use it to spin stories that sometimes touch on the surreal. My work is heavily influenced by the poetry of Frank O'Hara, who once said "What is happening to me, allowing for lies and exaggerations (which I try to avoid), goes into my poems".

The poems in this folio, allowing for a few exaggerations, articulate the speaker's here and now. The here is, nominally California, but also the speaker's idiosyncratic view of their world. California is filtered through his lexicon of vernacular, landscapes, and collected things. They manifest a persona and include kitchen-sink elements. By mixing the speaker's real world with the surreal, I am creating a refined form of surrealism. While they delve into the unconscious of the speaker, they are still approachable poems, in that the unconscious and the surreal are woven into a story.

The stories in these poems are about loss and the speaker's attempt to explain loss. The speaker stops along his journey to observe and reflect on their world, turning observations into something personal. The transition from collected things to an attempt to explain loss creates movement, and is similar to Ralph Waldo Emerson's idea of transition—the movement from one state or condition to another. Emerson argued that the quality of imagination is to flow, not freeze. Emerson wrote of fluidity in the universe, that permanence is just a matter of degrees. He distrusted stasis (a state of static balance or equilibrium during which little or no evolutionary change occurs), and that distrust of stasis is what gives us transitional poetry: the evolution to a different or altered state. The poems in this folio evolve from collected things to an altered state of consciousness; a surreal collage that spins stories of loss.

It's Not Easy Being a Moth

Almost-butterfly. Spanish Moon. Chinese Luna.
Tiny scales diffracting light. Rub the wings

and illusion dissolves into fingertips.
You are here on a whim, a woman hued

because you slipped saying I love you first, landing
a season early. No one pays attention in the beginning—

threads from fibers of maguey plant,
the excessive number of sewing needles.

I wear the cotón instead of shirts, loincloth instead
of pants. Feet bare, no shoes. At night we sleep

in patterns of checkered embroidered pearls
you stitched from sultepeque cotton.

And this bruise I got trying on new hats?
I'm still waiting to see how we emerge.

After You Drove

from Ojai to the foot of Adobe Hill,
found the Chumash Kohsho near a grove

of sycamores, you came home and said
everything I taught you was a lie.

You believe in sympathetic magic—
rattle carved of coyote bone to cure

crowning teeth. Hawk feather halos
stitched from fiber of milkweed

adorned with glass beads. Keep a cache
of polished charmstones for casting spells.

But California summers, all the hills dying
in pieces. Little ponds on little ranches

bake dry. Santa Ana gusts dust chaparral to
shades of buff-brown, the air sick with sage,

brush and scrub rolling down the arroyos.
I worry. Over sidewalk stains from walnut

shrubs in our front yard, August brushfires
scorching the shake roof, sea-cliffs eroding

along the Palisades. You pick a mackerel's eye
from the claw of a crab and make-believe

it's a pearl. Swim with speckled sea snakes
in Morro Bay. Lay low, conjure me down.

Hueneme

HOME

Today you are moving to Mendocino,
your van packed with twelve pairs

of well-pressed khaki slacks, assorted
collared shirts, and the totem I found

the year you were born—
a rock with a hole in it

just like the rock the Chinook woman
clung to, her arms passing right through

the middle. I read you all the wrong
bedtime stories – Kappas luring

children to drowning deaths,
crab-fish Krakens spurting brine

from dreadful nostrils. Once, we
emptied a tidal pool of sea urchins,

but I never decorated your room
in abalone shells. I should have changed

you into a dolphin, taught you how to hold
your breath, whispered *Hueneme* in your ear.

Parsimony

On San Nicolas Island, indigenous men used cactus thorns
to carve the universe on their wives until the women bled,
then applied mezcal to produce blue tattoos etched
from eyebrow to breast. Women who wore shell beads

the colors of beginning-dawn sky. It is much later now,
I am married, and my wife tells me she never
had a lover who said you are fine which makes me feel
guilty for all the Rorschach tests answered I just see ink.

Forgive me. And all the other husbands who wear
hip waders, go surf fishing at Leo Carrillo State Beach
to avoid long conversations. Husbands who keep secrets—

    where to collect the best perch baits
of mussel and ghost shrimp.

    Channel Islands are out there somewhere
you just can't see them for the fog.

    Power plant smokestacks at Morro Bay never find
their way into picture postcards.

    The human body sheds six hundred thousand skin
cells every day but you never lose sight of a tattoo—

scars too deep to be erased by a woman's own flesh.

FATHER'S DAY

Since my youngest son moved to another town, all my dowsing tip finds is salty water. It happens like that, in the middle years a father sleeps,

resigned because he can see the Sunday when he wants to swim off the island. And that makes the father sand because even if he breathes

nothing without scent of ocotillo, dry storms still wear thorns down. He starts packing boxes full of bird-bone pendants and abalone dishes.

Red ochre, glass fragments. A never-used harpoon tip. Soapstone ornaments and sandstone abraders. Subsists on raw shell fish and fat

of whale, his fondness for new potatoes, vegetables and fresh fruit waning. The father begins to dress in skins and feathers of sea scoters he stitches

together with sinews of seal, using bone needles that arrive in mail without a Father's Day card. Stops speaking any known language.

Postcard From Morro Bay

In a box of things you left behind—
sea urchin, slug, snail (extremes of low life)
I found a postcard addressed to me
without a stamp. On the front
is a picture of a man on a surfboard
holding an umbrella in his left hand.
Which is odd because the easiest way to keep
from getting wet is to avoid the ocean.
You can make someone believe
anything with a postcard. *Having a good time
wish you were here* that time you sent one from
Morro Bay. You tried to coax me
let's try cliff diving, you said *let's jump off Morro Rock.*
An inveterate matter to you, the distance
between sea and sky. You knew I was afraid
of heights, but still you teased me,
suggesting a trip even farther up the coast
to San Simeon, maybe Big Sur.
I could never go that high.
So I stayed home, alone, at sea level
digging holes in the sand. Burying myself.
Along came a tide and I disappeared.

Pamela Uschuk

Photo: Lucinda Luvaas

At my best, I write in a trance, drunk on the sounds of words, surfing the arc of imagery that fires emotion. Writing poetry is not schematic, not planned-out. I am compelled to write, to immerse in metaphor. A poem pulls me into another dimension that forms itself, spinning deeper and deeper its shape, colors and feelings, a super-nova of sorts exploring the inner-workings of issues or relationships that concern me. Writing poetry often is an ecstatic experience. When I write poems, my spirit expands forward and back, stretches sideways, explodes, reassembles. I learn. Poetry is memory's cortex. Poetry is duende. Poetry is primal connection. Poems mine me emotionally and spiritually.

The act of writing poetry is revolutionary in its reveletory discovery.

I don't write from prompts. I write in my journal daily. When I don't write for a period of time, I am restless as a lizard on a hot brick, out of balance.

Sound, rhythm and music are shamanic powers. When I was three, my father taught me the poem, "The Night Before Christmas," which I recited for all my relatives. It was easy to memorize because I, like many children, loved rhymes. I grew up in an immigrant home, hearing the music of several languages. Sound, rhyme and music are membranes to other dimensions. Poems carry us through those membranes into the imagination, that boundless dimension where anything and everything is possible.

For me, meaning, metaphor, sound, craft and emotion must work together in a poem or it fails. Although I respect them, I do not write language poems. Craft comes from meticulous revision. My poems yearn for healing—from disease, war, violence, betrayals, lies and loss. My poems seek justice and balance. Healing is found in the natural world, in community, in family, in the importance of ritual, in friendship, in courage, in the recogniton we are all inter-dependent. Healing is, ultimately, love. We are all part of one another's stories, one another's songs. When I say "we," I include animals, insects, plants, trees, mountains, oceans, the stars, planets and earth herself.

Shapeshifter

Each day I climb onto the broad shoulders of fear, tape
my fingers to fragile reins, weaving them through
its unpredictable and angry mane.

The Unknown is a cracked ice cube
popping when plunked in the imagination's
glass of clear water. Chemo's breath stinks,
could take my life with no regrets.

Fear is a shapeshifter with bloody teeth
or no teeth at all, just a broken jaw of anxiety.
Its arms are bruised from holding
too tight to the future's seductive promises.
What ifs are its favorite cuisine.

No one can predict how fear can jump
up from a birthday cake or laugh
like a monkey on fire or a horse starving for grain.

Fear grinds down the raw ore of the heart,
smelting each nodule of grief, removing
its aggregate shield. *I have to make you sick
to make you well,* the oncologist says,
scour each cell of your abdomen clean.

Watching Rikki Sculpt Clay
At Ghost Ranch

Hair a waterfall of night, Clay woman raises her throat, a coyote
praying to hands that shape her long micaceous skirt draped
over what grows insider her, delicate hands
carving out beauty in a world scarred by careless wounds.

Her intent is kind, digging earth stories undefiled. Form
finds itself in infinite design divined from the quick flames of making.
Slipping through her fingers, the ghosts of wolves
play snowy notes on flutes fashioned from their own thick bones.

She selects the slimmest blade to cut a hole in the vase
for spirit to escape as owl breath, as smoke,
as wind opening spaces between
the brittle branches of winter pines.

Clay woman holds her hands over her skirt,
over the amniotic sommersault of her child to be,
this sea of beginnings washed by the light
sculpting sandstone's fantastic alchemy.

Lifting a basket of fresh-picked sage, Clay woman tucks
a twig over her ear to perfume the day, spins
on hope's mineral wheel, her heart a constellation
in the Milky Way, shaping her story as she waits.

Endangered Species

For Judi Uschuk-Stahl and Roy Orozco

In Costa Rica, our park guide, a muralist, says
the red-backed squirrel money is extinct,
gone the one monkey I'd flown thousands
of miles for, its creamy face sweet as white chocolate
after summer's diet of chewing bitter leaves.

This dense canopy of figs and marvelous trees
hosts millions of diverse nations—bromeilliads
and vines, trees trunk dripping color like smooth
elephant legs dipped in tie-dyed neons.

Done whoop-roaring by nine a.m., howler monkeys
drape arms and legs over high limbs to snooze
having chewed too many hallucinogens.
In altered states above the commerce of our lives,
they'll dream away the heated day.

At the beach, Capuchins squat on lithe black legs
scouting treats in the sweaty hands of tourists.
Their alabaster faces are wise in the ways of theft
and self-sustainability. Deft, a monkey swoops to snatch
a teen's bag of chips with fingertips as delicate as breath.

My sister would have liked it here close to the Equator,
would have thrown back her mahogany hair, thrilled
as I by the bright red and black Halloween crabs
big as my face crawling the rainforest floor
or the black hawk hanging drenched wings
over its leaf-lit perch. I remember her fountain laugh,

the way she chuckled at me where two contrails
crossed a sundog just a week after her death, saying
"From this great distance, everything looks
funny down there." Released from her wheelchair,
she ran through thunderheads to stop my tears.

When Roy shakes his head at the disappearance
of squirrel monkeys from the medicine world, I think
how we are all endangered. It's not been a month since
my sister vanished with her unblemished skin and last dusky breath.
Not one of us expected her to leave. I can hardly bear
the sultry sun, the stun of blue ocean or the sweet child
trying to feed that Capuchin a piece of his banana.

Back at the hotel, I chill, snap photos of blue trumpet flowers
for friends. Their petals widen for attention.
Next, I frame Roy's mural, a mélange of scarlet macaws
bloodying sky above the trees, a three-toed sloth with Li Po's face,
and, above Roy's signature, a red-backed squirrel monkey
staring for eternity at a chlorinated swimming pool.

It is then what appears to be a small bag of groceries
tumbles through banana leaves past my head.
I cringe, squint at iridescent fur
orange as a courtesan's skirt, the creamy furred face
questioning mine, while its disoriented body climbs into full view.
Unconcerned with me, the monkey is either unmistakably alive
or a palpable ghost. Roy's painting comes true.

What had been extinct is close as my hand,
mumbling the language of time and memory.
Neither of us can look away, gauging the other.
When I call for my husband and his camera,
the monkey is undeterred, poses for shots as if to say
I'm here. I'm
here, alive as you.

I can almost touch the glowing fur, the fiery
mantle vital, resurrection
in a jungle tangled with hope's endangered leaves.

Toward Wings

Between sleep and what I assume to be real, I pick up the old sword
cutting fat from wounds sewn together with the raw sinews of fear.
I remember flying from my horse atop the Kyber Pass,
my brother charging, heartbroken and fierce to avenge my death.
This time I pull the spear from my chest,
cauterize that terrible wound with burning feathers,
the hooked beak of the eagle buoyed by wind.

Dreams are a way out as much as a way in to the labyrinth.
Since surgery, my dreams are black velvet fists curled
sleeping in sacred rooms. Sutured as those layered incisions
closing deep wounds, they refuse to open.

Where did they throw the tumors, my cancered womb,
cervix, fallopian tubes?
The ovaries that bloomed disease?

Fear grows like basil in a pot spun of anxiety and loathing.
Stop watering it with tears, and it dies.
No little violins play.
Little violins recall the scalpel. The trick
is not to listen to pity clinging to their strings.

A black-chinned hummingbird drops from the dead Saguaro arm
to the pink-mouthed blossom for nectar, drinks
deep through its messenger beak.

Sun reaches through monsoon clouds, blades of light,
pulling me skyward, toward
wings I cannot see.

Song of Reprieve

for Reggie Arthur

Desert broom sweeps sky clean, sweeps
the orange songs of goldfinches and warblers
into its branches, hallelujahs of joy.
Feathers, too, are small brooms grooming air
we navigate to breathe.

I push aside pain, thin and screeching
like slices of mica under tires, my lessons
old as lizards whose ancestors slid
under the booming feet of brontosaurus
grazing the high branches of rain forest trees
that time and memory morphed into this desert.

Pain redirects the arc of my arms and legs
in their simple intent of motion.
The suffering of lizards is fully as sharp as my own.

On Losing a Mother

for Joy

Face West.
This is the doorway open for the leap.
Know the protocols, chants, food that loves her.

Bathe what shrinks, the disappearing length of her arms,
ankles, the feet each hour more lucent than the hour before.
Watch the ark of the chest as it fills with dusk,
the way breath must darken as it leaves.

You've driven hundreds of miles to find her
amid the stained sheets of childhood,
tangled in wool blankets and bedsores.
She smiles, wants biscuits and gravy for breakfast.
The morphine drips.

It is the same song repeating itself across the globe,
the way we circle one another like elephants
comforting a wounded sister or like water
that doubles back to eat its own corpse.

This is the body of the blood you feasted on
as a fetus orbiting inside her womb. You
are her singing in a winter kitchen
when love forgot the keys to the house,
her breath, her light,
her dark tears.

To say goodbye, stroke her hair gone to silver wire,
her bare arms. Listen,
even though she has lost her voice,
speaks now only with her eyes
that hold each trembling leaf of you.

Hold her hand, place
your heart over her heart
to absorb the dual cadence, a cappella devotional,
sheet music of the unsaid you've come to understand.

Who is your witness? Your sister and your brother
hover over her bed. Her eyes open
the color of deep sea water seeping
into the cenote of your own wild places. Her eyes
see beyond the shadows her children make.

Ready yourself for her leap.
It will surprise you no matter
how many times you've practiced in your head.
Leaving is like this, a wrenching away to peace.

Turn inside her as she turns
to the throbbing inside a ceremonial drum,
a song of honor for your mother
dying in all her perfect imperfections.

Air is filling her bones, turning them into birds,
into reed flutes, just as sure as her spirit fills the room
where you have prepared all of her favorite foods.

Publication Credits

Tanya Ko Hong

"*Heo Nanseolhean (1563-1589)," *Paris Press Spiraling Poetry*, 2015

"Grandmother Talking Camptowns," *Paris Press Spiraling Poetry*, 2015

"Oxtail Soup," *Paris Press Spiraling Poetry*, 2015

"Comfort Woman," *Beloit Poetry Journal*, 2014

"The War Still Inside You," *Entropy*, 2017

"Gacela of Moonshine," *Two Hawks Quarterly*, 2012

Raymond Gibson

"Glass", *First Literary Review-East's* May 2015 issue

Cynthia Atkins

"The Street Is A Museum", *Gamut Magazine*

"God Is A Library", *Sundog Lit*

"Graffiti Is My Mother", *Gargoyle Magazine*

"Family Therapy (II)", *The Florida Review*

"Zig-Zag", *Sou'wester*

"God Is The Myth", *Gamut Magazine*

Jennifer Martelli

"The Nightingale and The Finch," *The Plath Poetry Project*, December 18, 2017

"The Sacrifice," *The Plath Poetry Project*, October 20, 2017

"Mal 'Occhio," *Arcturus (The Chicago Review of Books)*, June, 2017

"Pluto's Heart is a White/Shadow," *White Stag (Psychologia)*, 2016

"Phoebe," *Topology*, May 2016

John James

"Years I've Slept Right Through," *Harpur Palate*

"History (n.)," *The Kenyon Review*

"Metamorphoses," *Boston Review*

"The Milk Hours," *The Louisville Review*

"Poem Around Which Everything Is Structured," *Meridian*

"Chthonic," *Best New Poets 2013*

Susan Berlin

"False Witness" and "Through the Funnel of a Loose Fist", *Mudfish.*

"The Armoire", *South Road.*

"Prayer", *Oberon.*

"Request Denied", *Atlanta Review.*

Mark Lee Webb

"After You Drove", *Ninth Letter*

"Father's Day", *Slippery Elm*

"Hueneme", *The Louisville Review*

"It's Not Easy Being a Moth", *RipRap*

"Parsimony", *JuxtaProse*

Contributor Notes

Jocelyn Heath is currently an Assistant Professor in English at Norfolk State University, having recently completed her creative PhD at Georgia State University. Her poem "Orbital" won the 2014 Alison Joseph Poetry Award from *Crab Orchard Review*. Her work has also appeared in *The Atlantic, Fourth River, Poet Lore, Sinister Wisdom, Bellingham Review, The National Poetry Review*, and other journals. She is an Assistant Editor for *Smartish Pace*, and has reviewed poetry for *Lambda Literary* and others.

Tanya (Hyonhye) Ko Hong, poet, translator and cultural curator, has been published in *Rattle, Beloit Poetry Journal, Entropy, Cultural Weekly, Korea Times, Korea Central Daily News*, and elsewhere. She has an MFA in creative writing from Antioch University Los Angeles, and is the author of four collections of poetry, most recently, *Mother to Myself*, A collection of poems in Korean (Prunsasang Press, 2015). Her poem, "Comfort Woman" got honorable mention in the 2015 Women's National Book Association. Tanya is an ongoing advocate of bilingual poetry, promoting the work of immigrant poets. She lives Palos Verdes, CA. www.tanyakohong.com

Raymond Gibson (b. 1980) earned his MFA in creative writing from Florida Atlantic University, and published two chapbooks with Glass Lyre Press. His work can be found in *White Stag, Gravel, Rust+Moth*, and *Ninth Letter*. He lives in Hollywood, Florida.

Cynthia Atkins was born and raised in Chicago, Il, receiving a an MFA from Columbia University's School of the Arts. She is the author of *Psyche's Weathers* and *In The Event of Full Disclosure*. Her poems have appeared in numerous journals, including, *Alaska Quarterly Review, BOMB, Cultural Weekly, Diode, Florida Review, Green Mountains Review, Harpur Palate, Hermeneutic Chaos, Le Zaporogue, North American Review, Seneca Review, Tampa Review, Valparaiso Review* and *Verse Daily*, among others. She currently teaches Creative Writing in the continuing Ed program at Blue Ridge Community College and lives on the Maury River of Rockbridge County, VA with the artist Phillip Welch and their family. More info and work at: www.cynthiatkins.com

Jennifer Martelli is the author of *The Uncanny Valley* (Big Table Publishing Company, 2016) and *My Tarantella* (forthcoming, Bordighera Press). Her work has appeared or will appear in *The Superstition Review, Sugar House, Thrush, Carve, Glass Poetry Journal, Cleaver, The Heavy Feather Review,* and *Tinderbox Poetry Journal*. Jennifer Martelli has been nominated for Pushcart and Best of the Net Prizes and is the recipient of the Massachusetts Cultural Council Grant in Poetry. She is the co-curator for *The Mom Egg* VOX Folio.

John James is the author of *Chthonic*, winner of the 2014 CutBank Chapbook Prize. His poems appear in *Boston Review, Kenyon Review, Gulf Coast, Poetry Northwest, Best American Poetry 2017,* and elsewhere. His first book manuscript, *The Milk Hours*, has been named a finalist for the National Poetry Series, Four Way Books' Levis Prize, the Crab Orchard First Book Award, and other honors. He splits his time between Washington, DC, and the San Francisco Bay Area, where he is pursuing a Ph.D. in English at the University of California, Berkeley.

Shadab Zeest Hashmi's latest work, *Ghazal Cosmopolitan*, has been praised by poet Marilyn Hacker as "a marvelous interweaving of poetry, scholarship, literary criticism and memoir." She has received the San Diego Book Award for poetry, the Nazim Hikmet Prize and multiple Pushcart nominations. Her poetry has been translated into Spanish and Urdu, and has appeared in anthologies and journals worldwide. Her books of poetry include *Baker of Tarifa* and *Kohl and Chalk*. She lives in San Diego and has taught in the MFA program at San Diego State University as a writer-in-residence.

Susan Berlin's poems have appeared in *Alaska Quarterly, Asheville Poetry Review, Atlanta Review, Cape Cod Poetry Review, Georgetown Review, Harvard Review, Mudfish, Naugatuck River Review, New Millennium Writings, Oberon* and *Ploughshares,* among many others. A multiple Pushcart Prize nominee and twice a finalist for the National Poetry Series, she was awarded First Prize in the Galway Kinnell Poetry Contest by the Rhode Island Council on the Arts She has received an International Publication Prize and International Merit Award from *Atlanta Review*. Her book, *The Same Amount of Ink*, was published by Glass Lyre Press in 2016. She lives in Yarmouth Port, MA.

Mark Lee Webb received his MFA from Queens University of Charlotte. He has published two chapbooks: *WHATEVERITS* (Finishing Line Press, 2014) and *THE WEIGHT of PAPER* (ELJ Publications, 2014). Mark's poems have appeared in many literary journals, including *Ninth Letter, Rattle, The Louisville Review, Soundings Review, Glassworks, Chiron Review, The Baltimore Review, RipRap,* and *Star 82 Review*.

Political activist and wilderness advocate, **Pam Uschuk** has howled out six books of poems, including *CRAZY LOVE,* winner of a 2010 American Book Award, *FINDING PEACHES IN THE DESERT* (Tucson/Pima Literaature Award), and her most recent, *BLOOD FLOWER,* one of Book List's Notable Books in 2015.

Translated into more than a dozen languages, her work appears in over three hundred journals and anthologies worldwide, including *Poetry, Ploughshares, Agni Review, Parnassus Review,* etc.

Among her awards are the War Poetry Prize from winningwrites.com, New Millenium Poetry Prize, Best of the Web, the Struga International Poetry Prize (for a theme poem), the Dorothy Daniels Writing Award from the National League of American PEN Women, the King's English Poetry Prize and prizes from Ascent, Iris, and Amnesty International.

Editor-In-Chief of *Cutthroat, A Journal Of The Arts,* Uschuk lives in Tucson, Arizona. She edited the anthology, *Truth to Power: Writers Respond To Rhetoric Of Hate And Fear.* Pam is often a featured writer at the Prague Summer Programs and at Ghost Ranch. She teaches at the University of Arizona's Poetry Center. In 2011, she held the John C. Hodges Visiting Writer Chair at University of Tennessee, Knoxville. She's finishing work on a multi-genre memoir called *Of Thunderlight And Moon: An Odyssey Through Ovarian Cancer.*

Glass Lyre Press

exceptional works to replenish the spirit

Glass Lyre Press is an independent literary publisher interested in technically accomplished, stylistically distinct, and original work. Glass Lyre seeks diverse writers that possess a dynamic aesthetic and an ability to emotionally and intellectually engage a wide audience of readers.

Glass Lyre's vision is to connect the world through language and art. We hope to expand the scope of poetry and short fiction for the general reader through exceptionally well-written books, which evoke emotion, provide insight, and resonate with the human spirit.

Poetry Collections
Poetry Chapbooks
Select Short & Flash Fiction
Anthologies

www.GlassLyrePress.com

www.ingramcontent.com/pod-product-compliance
Lightning Source LLC
Chambersburg PA
CBHW021155080526
44588CB00008B/346